M000211304

THE
TAURUS
ORACLE

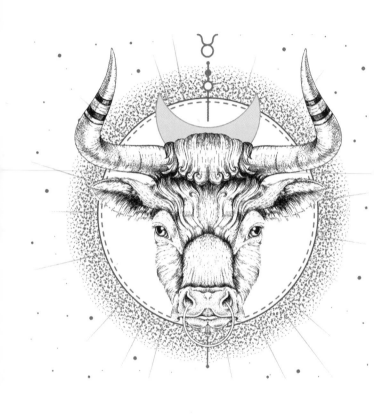

THE
TAURUS
ORACLE

INSTANT ANSWERS FROM
YOUR COSMIC SELF

STELLA FONTAINE

greenfinch

Introduction

Welcome to your zodiac oracle,
carefully crafted especially for you
Taurus, and brimming with the
wisdom of the universe.

Is there a tricky-to-answer question niggling at you and you need an answer?

Whenever you're unsure whether to say 'yes' or 'no', whether to go back or to carry on, whether to trust or to turn away, make some time for a personal session with your very own oracle. Drawing on your astrological profile, your zodiac oracle will guide you in understanding, interpreting and answering those burning questions that life throws your way. Discovering your true path will become an enlightening journey of self-actualization.

Humans have long cast their eyes heavenwards to seek answers from the universe. For millennia the sun, moon and stars have been our constant companions as they repeat their paths and patterns across the skies. We continue to turn to the cosmos for guidance, trusting in the deep and abiding wisdom of the universe as we strive for fulfilment, truth and understanding.

The most basic and familiar aspect of astrology draws on the twelve signs of the zodiac, each connected to a unique constellation as well as its own particular colours, numbers and characteristics. These twelve familiar signs are also known as the sun signs: Aries, Taurus, Gemini, Cancer, Leo, Virgo, Libra, Scorpio, Sagittarius, Capricorn, Aquarius and Pisces.

Aries   Taurus   Gemini   Cancer   Leo   Virgo

Libra   Scorpio   Sagittarius   Capricorn   Aquarius   Pisces

Each sign is associated with an element (fire, air, earth or water), and also carries a particular quality: cardinal (action-takers), fixed (steady and constant) and mutable (changeable and transformational). Beginning to understand these complex combinations, and to recognize the layered influences they bring to bear on your life, will unlock your own potential for personal insight, self-awareness and discovery.

In our data-flooded lives, now more than ever it can be difficult to know where to turn for guidance and advice. With your astrology oracle always by your side, navigating life's twists and turns will become a smoother, more mindful process. Harness the prescience of the stars and tune in to the resonance of your sun sign with this wisdom-packed guide that will lead you to greater self-knowledge and deeper confidence in the decisions you are making. Of course, not all questions are created equal; your unique character, your circumstances and the issues with which you find yourself confronted all add up to a conundrum unlike any other... but with your question in mind and your zodiac oracle in your hand, you're already halfway to the answer.

Taurus

APRIL 20 TO MAY 20

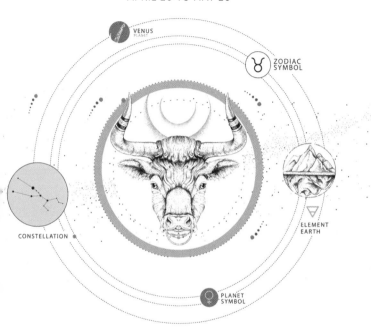

Element: Earth

Quality: Fixed

Named for the constellation: Taurus (the bull)

Ruled by: Venus

Opposite: Scorpio

Characterized by: Devotion, reliability, patience

Colour: Green, pink

How to Use This Book

You can engage with your oracle whenever you need to but, for best results, create an atmosphere of calm and quiet, somewhere you will not be disturbed, making a place for yourself and your question to take priority. Whether this is a particular physical area you turn to in times of contemplation, or whether you need to fence off a dedicated space within yourself during your busy day, that all depends on you and your circumstances. Whichever you choose, it is essential that you actively put other thoughts and distractions to one side in order to concentrate upon the question you wish to answer.

Find a comfortable position, cradle this book lightly in your hands, close your eyes, centre yourself. Focus on the question you wish to ask. Set your intention gently and mindfully towards your desire to answer this question, to the exclusion of all other thoughts and mind-chatter. Allow all else to float softly away, as you remain quiet and still, gently watching the shape and form of the question you wish to address. Gently deepen and slow your breathing.

Tune in to the ancient resonance of your star sign, the vibrations of your surroundings, the beat of your heart and the flow of life and the universe moving in and around you. You are one with the universe.

Now simply press the book between your palms as you clearly and distinctly ask your question (whether aloud or in your head), then open it at any page. Open your eyes. Your advice will be revealed.

Read it carefully. Take your time turning this wisdom over in your mind, allowing your thoughts to surround it, to absorb it, flow with it, then to linger and settle where they will.

Remember, your oracle will not provide anything as blunt and brutal as a completely literal answer. That is not its role. Rather, you will be gently guided towards the truth you seek through your own consciousness, experience and understanding. And as a result, you will grow, learn and flourish.

Let's begin.

Close your eyes.

Hold the question you want
answered clearly in your mind.

Open your oracle to any page to
reveal your cosmic insight.

A little Taurean self-love never goes amiss, and it might be time for some nourishment (whether for the soul or the body, or both...). Take it back to the kitchen Taurus, and let's see what's cooking.

When you know what it is you really want, there is nothing more powerful than that absolute determination Taurus is so famous for.

Compromise is always possible, but you will need to follow the path of least resistance. As a peace-loving bull, with Venus on your side, this shouldn't be too difficult for you.

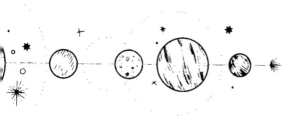

Your even-paced approach
seems sensible to you, of course it
does. But perhaps you are just seeing
the obvious on this one. Try looking at
it from another angle (or two) in case
you've missed something.

Other people may take
longer to adjust to change than
you do Taurus, and your easy
adaptability might cause envy.
Empathy is key right now.

No one can deny it's always easier to stick to the safe questions, but is this really the question you want an answer to right now? Give it a little more thought, be brave and ask again.

Others sometimes describe your approach as stubborn (the very idea!), when in fact you know perfectly well that it is pure dedication, and they are likely simply envious of your work ethic. Concern yourself less with how other people see this issue; be loyal to yourself.

Take a few moments today to
pause and reflect in your beloved
natural surroundings – the answer will
reveal itself. This is a tricky one, but
not for the reasons you
might first think.

Go easy on fault-finding (with others as well as yourself). Dial down that thinking brain and allow your gut instinct to direct you on this one.

Clever and ambitious as you are, sometimes you need to take a pause and look around while you wait for the world to catch up. There is something you still need to know.

Your Taurean drive and ambition
might not have served you well on
this occasion – it is important to
investigate further. The details are
not exactly as they might have
seemed at the beginning.

Although it doesn't quite fit
with that ordered way you like to
run your life, this time you need to
acknowledge that there are several
potential outcomes.

Relinquishing control can feel irresponsible – after all, surely you will do this best. But learn to trust your stars; the path ahead is all lit up, ready for you to follow.

Change is on its way. It is not time to
start planning, much as you would love
to. But be receptive to the signs and
remain open to possibilities.

Your Taurus desire to get your point across, no matter what, will not necessarily help you win this time. Worry less about what other people are thinking (and don't obsess over the fact that they are clearly wrong); you cannot control the feelings of others. They will come to realize the truth in time.

Play the long game and keep your
powder dry. A sequence of small wins
is the secret to success.

With Scorpio as your opposite sign,
sometimes you need to remember
that a sting in the tail can be a
powerful last resort Taurus.
Now is one of those
times.

Patience and persistence
come naturally to you, they are
such steadfast components of your
Taurus nature. These characteristics
will be the key again this time.

Your fullest potential is not to
be found in the pursuit of material
things, but in nurturing the richness of
your internal life. Try to acknowledge
that same value in those around you.

A more comprehensive understanding will help simplify your approach. Don't allow yourself to be distracted from the task at hand. Time devoted to expanding your learning is never wasted.

Admired as one of the hardest-working signs, now it's time to make the most of your Taurus talents. Do not shy away from this challenge. Nothing worth doing seems easy at first.

Your first impulse was the right one, although initially it may have seemed to make little sense. Quiet your analytical brain and go with it.

It will not be the easiest path, but this is the one you are destined to travel. Head down, one foot in front of the other and carry on.

Your determined approach can sometimes trap you into too steady a pace. Uncertain times call for decisive action; choose your path and get moving.

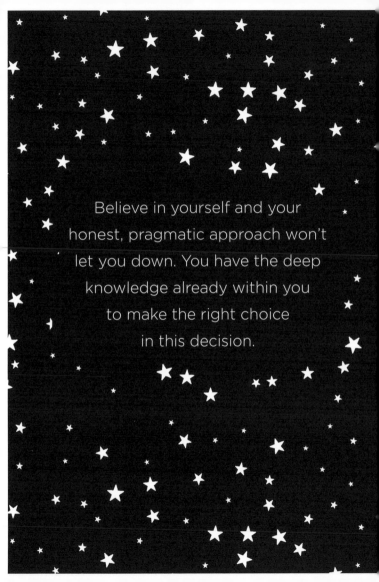

Believe in yourself and your
honest, pragmatic approach won't
let you down. You have the deep
knowledge already within you
to make the right choice
in this decision.

Relax and allow things
to be as they are. The small
things have a way of working
themselves out, you know.

Much as you hate to do this
Taurus, it might be time to change
your thinking on this matter; there is a
small chance that you might be wrong.
At least consider the possibility.

Power struggles do crop up for you every now and again, especially when an authority figure or another source of rule-making or control is involved. Take it easy on yourself, and on them, and remember that you don't have to charge straight ahead into whatever you perceive the problem to be. Find a way around, rather than confronting this head on.

Despite your well-known honesty and reputation for giving excellent advice, this might be one of those situations in which actions speak louder than words.

Although you pride yourself on your harmonious relationships, now and again a sticky situation does find its way to your door. Resist the temptation to scramble for an instant solution; just watch and wait.

Asserting yourself calmly and
with confidence will enable others to
more fully understand your viewpoint
and come to their own conclusions.
This is vital if you are to achieve a
clear and fair outcome.

Affirm your need for enough time to make your decisions or produce a result Taurus. Rushing this will only create the need for more work later. Slow and steady is the way to go.

Keep your feet firmly planted
on the ground Taurus. As an Earth
sign, it is even more important for you
than most that you maintain an even
and secure base. Don't allow yourself
to be swept up in the excitement
of fantasy.

Adopting a philosophical approach and a willingness to compromise will be of enormous benefit to you in the days and weeks ahead. You might even align your goals with someone or something you currently consider an obstacle. Your heart (and your stress levels) will thank you.

Make the most of this opportunity
to exercise your compassion Taurus.
Set any impatience aside.

Usually you are so in charge Taurus, it can feel very disorienting when things seem not to be going your way. But, as ever, there is a greater plan at work here. Breathe, stay in the moment, try to let go of that you are seeking to hold and this too shall pass.

Imagination and creativity will
be your steadfast helpers on this
journey. Be careful not to let your
tendency to stick to the process send
you off course – this demands
a different approach.

Such a powerful Earth sign,
you know better than most the
benefit of keeping those feet firmly
planted. Let the ground beneath
support and lift you as you reach
for the stars.

Now, we all know that you adore indulgence and self-love comes naturally to you. Pull back from all those commitments and duties, and sink into a deep, fragrant bath, prepare the food you are really craving (and take the time to enjoy it), or book yourself in for your favourite massage. You deserve it.

It's time to get a blast of fresh air around that big, hard-working Taurus brain of yours; powerful medicine for everyone, of course, but no one loves a nature tonic better than you. Head for the sea, climb that hill or take a long, leisurely stroll through a forest.

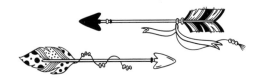

Of course, anything is possible, especially for a clever Taurus. But you might need to consider the viewpoints of others this time. The direction of approach will make all the difference.

The involvement of others can over-complicate things sometimes - it would be much more efficient if you could do it yourself, of course. But you are patient and understanding (usually...) and you know it's not their fault they don't have your Taurus talents. Allow others to help.

Be sure everyone has the same view of a shared project before you conclude and finalize arrangements.

Retreat into your own space to nurture yourself with relaxation, nourishment and rest. A healthy bull is a happy bull and stretching yourself too thin means you run the risk of something snapping Taurus.

Bearing a grudge is a particular Taurus skill and your ability hold onto that resentment longer and with greater determination than most is a point of pride. However, with an eye on the greater good, you need to forgive mistakes that have been made. Forgiving doesn't mean forgetting but moving on is the only practical option here.

Trust your intuition to generate
a few sparky connections for you; this
one is more complicated than what
you can see on the surface.

You are loyal, patient, determined
and the most brilliant company. But
you will only keep bringing your best
game if you allow your energy to
replenish. Commit to some downtime
today and you'll be ready to face the
world again in no time.

Time to screw your courage to the sticking place and choose the right question. Your answer will lie right in front of you the minute you are brave enough to ask.

Follow your gut instinct on this one;
your first impression was correct.

Comprehensive solution-crafting
and plan-instigation are second nature
to you Taurus. But the decision to aim
for a big change will not come easily
and is best not made on the spur
of the moment. Take the time
this requires.

You are what you do, not what you say. Empty words and hollow promises are not your style, don't be tempted to sidestep your impulse to maintain integrity – it has never failed you yet.

Speaking your truth, while important to you, is not always the keenest path to cementing relationships. Remember that everyone sees things through their own eyes. Suspend judgement and, if you must have your say, consider all likely outcomes first.

A long journey is about to come to an end Taurus. All you have invested, and the care you have taken, will soon pay off.

Trust those who tell you what you need to hear... Loyalty and truth go together on this one. Set ego aside.

Take the necessary steps to get what you want Taurus. Only you can truly know what matters to you.

Stand your ground Taurus.
Use the solidity of your bullish
personality to hold the space you
require in this situation. Don't move
on until you are ready.

Not all obstacles have to be grappled with; of course, your first impulse is to lower your bullish horns and head straight for the problem. But stepping around it rather than becoming tangled in a sticky situation is often a more elegant solution.

Keep a strong handle on the things you need to do to stay balanced. As an Earth sign, it is vital that you stay grounded. Connect with nature and movement, fresh water and green spaces. Above all, be kind to yourself.

There is a difference
between friendship and flattery.
Not all signs are gifted with your
dedication to plain-speaking and some
are more focused on easing their own
path than acknowledging truth.
Remember this.

Self-doubt will not help you on
this occasion; resist second-guessing
yourself. Your personal clarity and
strength of purpose will
serve you well.

If circumstances look too difficult, press pause and disengage, even for a short time. A little distance will make all the difference.

Retaining a measured approach and taking a step back is vital. Very rarely is an immediate response actually required; do not allow the flustered approach of others to panic you. Take your time in coming to your decision, in classic Taurus style.

Your success will depend on doing the very thing that looks right but feels counterintuitive. Let your head take precedence over your heart on this one.

Take a break from inside your
head for a while Taurus, and leave
your own issues to one side. You have
been so caught up in personal
situations recently you might not
have noticed that someone else
could really use a hand.

Circumstances might not
be quite as they seem – adopt
a measured Taurean approach
and take another look.

Don't be daunted by what might look like a big or overwhelming task or project Taurus. With your trademark calm and pragmatic approach, you will easily cope with this.

Forthcoming events may well force a decision requiring you to commit to growth. This is a wonderful opportunity, embrace it.

A shift might suddenly expose underlying issues of hurt or confusion. While potentially painful at first, you should embrace the opportunity to deal with these now as a true blessing.

Pastures new lie just over the horizon Taurus; make the extra effort to reach them and greater satisfaction and happiness will result.

What you project is what others receive; they cannot know what is in your heart unless you explain it to them.

Difficulties teach lessons that will benefit your approach in the future. What comes next is entirely in your hands. Learn from the past and move on.

Reshape any irritation at the current situation into compassion, Taurus. If anyone can do this, it's you.

Responsible and self-sacrificing, it is also important that you receive the recognition you deserve (both for the sake of your ego and for the record). You are not often overlooked, but don't miss out on an opportunity to own your achievements this time.

You will find a way Taurus, and there are plenty of options. Take an easier route this time if you can.

Perseverance is certainly one of your star-given virtues, even if you can't always see where the hard work might be leading you. But do bear in mind that people are different and most probably need an idea of where their reward might lie in order to knuckle down and get on with it.

It is never too late

for an apology.

Resist your Taurus urge to take control of this situation – there are several players to consider. Of course, you would do it best, with the most robust attention to detail and a pragmatic eye on outcomes, but allow all the options. The right one will soon become clear.

Don't be too suspicious of an easy win this time, even if it feels like it's not all it should be. Something much more difficult is just around the corner, you can sink your teeth into that soon.

Others might have caught a glimpse of what they are labelling a 'bad temper' (the very idea...), but of course all you want to do is protect the hard work and thought you have already invested. Be careful to harness the best parts of your Taurean nature, to help you push through this one. And stay out of china shops for a while.

Find a way to carry on, even if
it wasn't part of your original plan.
Slowing your pace at this point will not
guarantee the greatest rewards.

Ambitious, tough-skinned
when it matters, hard-working
and success-driven – that's all classic
Taurus. But don't forget that softer,
more vulnerable part. You don't have
to pretend that bullishness is the real
you all the time. Take a chance
and open up.

There is a chance you are over-mixing this one. Be mindful that your attempts to make sure this is done properly aren't misinterpreted as unnecessarily complicated or time-consuming.

Even though it goes against your best Taurean instincts (which infinitely prefer calm and security), sometimes you need to allow the risk of chaos in order to give yourself the chance of a big success. Being too stubborn to try at all will be the real failure – don't let that happen.

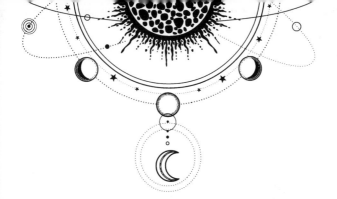

Your skills-repertoire is more
than comprehensive enough to meet
the chances presenting themselves.
This opportunity could well have been
crafted especially for you.

Slow down for the time being – even though it might feel like something must be done immediately, set your impatience aside on this one. You will know when the time is right.

Your Taurus talents for perfect planning and spotting potential pitfalls will be in great demand. Time to look ahead and focus on the future.

Truth and wisdom are more
likely to reveal themselves if you allow
yourself the peace and solitude to
see clearly. Silence and space are
imperative if you are going to
sort this one out.

Pull yourself together from the core, shake off that nervous energy and engage with structure, clarity and intention. Stand tall and be present in the moment.

Emotions may be running
ragged and tempers flaring around
you Taurus, but keep your cool. Your
renowned Taurean balance and calm
will set a fine example for others.

Avoid potential frustration by keeping body and mind clean and balanced Taurus. Exercise, enough sleep and good food will all be tremendously beneficial.

You are ruled by Venus, bringing
beauty and love into your life.
Understand that these are a gift and
not everyone is as lucky as you.

Your patience and loyalty are beyond reproach, and you are loving, supportive and usually content Taurus. Guard against your darker tendencies, as they may lead you into stubbornness or even jealousy. Nothing good will come of those.

You will achieve the very best results by speaking from the heart, with compassion and understanding for those you are addressing.

You are usually even-tempered and so steady-paced, it can be a shock to those around you when you finally see red and charge like the bull you are. Console yourself that it doesn't happen terribly often, or without provocation.

Taurus is an Earth sign and so you are happiest outdoors, serene and surrounded by nature. Keep this self-knowledge in your back pocket and draw on it as your first response when you start to feel any signs of stress or being overwhelmed. Nature will recalibrate and reset your soul.

A pleasure-loving sign, you love to
be pampered. You work hard, but
relax even harder, and so you should.
If some of the other signs took a leaf
out of your book on this one now
and again, the world would be a
much more peaceful place.
Indulge yourself.

Keeping your horizons tight and your hopes and dreams small only limits your own potential Taurus. Think bigger.

A practical, patient and consistent sign, you gain great pleasure from the knowledge that you are carefully, steadily working towards a reliable goal. Just be careful that the satisfaction you gain from planning for the future isn't at the expense of enjoyment you could experience today. After all, who can really say what tomorrow may bring?
Carpe diem, Taurus.

You are a happy bull
Taurus, trustworthy and devoted
(if very occasionally a little obstinate).
Be careful that your dedication and
loyalty don't encourage a tendency
to linger longer than you should in
an unproductive or unhealthy
situation; there are some
things even you can't fix.

Hold on a little bit longer Taurus,
the time is not yet right.

It's important that you are honest
with yourself and others, on this
occasion especially; self-knowledge
is never a weakness.

Your habit is to hold on, stand firm and maintain a steadfast approach. But there is nothing more to be gained with this one, staying longer than anyone else will not win you any points.

You like to enjoy the very best Taurus, and you love to be properly, deeply comfortable. But don't take stability too far and let your options grow stagnant; risk is necessary once in a while if you want a chance at those big rewards.

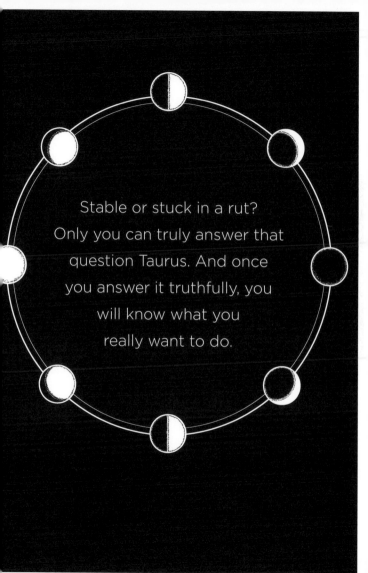

Stable or stuck in a rut?
Only you can truly answer that
question Taurus. And once
you answer it truthfully, you
will know what you
really want to do.

With a little support and instruction, you will find it much simpler than you feared to conquer a creative dream you have been toying with of late. Explore all avenues to find the resources you need to help you.

Love holds the answer
to this one Taurus.

Feedback is not always required;
true and concentrated listening is a
rare and valuable skill.

The choices you make inevitably have a knock-on effect for those whose lives are interconnected with yours. Obviously, you can't control the outcome for everyone, but be sure you consider the likely repercussions before you take a step you won't be able to undo.

Look for the middle ground – although the options may seem exciting, you don't want to end up biting off more than you can chew.

Ensure that others feel heard when they engage with you. Give the gift of your focussed attention.

Stability and gentleness sit comfortably with you, and all around you benefit. Just make sure that you are receiving enough in return to continue your own growth and to feel nurtured.

Supposedly a materialistic
sign, it is time to put your worth and
possessions to good use. Acquisitions
and material wealth are of no value in
and of themselves – your best step
right now would be to enrich your
family and community in some way.

Prosperity and wealth can
be measured in more than just
material possessions; count love, luck
and belonging among your
treasures Taurus.

Be careful not to damage someone else with your anger or frustration at your own inability to act in the way you would like to. Take this one step at a time and be mindful of your own strength and forcefulness. Tone it down a bit lest you accidentally hit someone you weren't even aiming for.

When a boost of energy comes
your way Taurus, be sure you make
the most of it. You will find that with
all your other talents already in place
you can get a whole lot done,
especially completing all those bits
and pieces you have been putting off
and making those decisions you
have been avoiding.

Adding a bit more focus to
your practice, whether work or
self-improvement, will reap big
rewards. Be sure not to push yourself
too hard though Taurus; add self-love
into the mix as well.

When things feel unpredictable and maybe a little wobbly, you can lean on those around you. They will appreciate knowing that you feel you can depend on them as much as they rely on you.

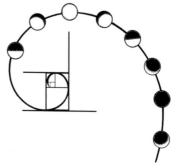

This is perhaps a better time to
appeal to the intellect rather than the
emotions of others. Spend time
explaining the logical facts, rather than
discussing feelings, and they will be
better able to understand
your position.

Ask for what you need, directly and clearly, without leaving any room for potential confusion or misunderstanding. Say it as it is, then reap the rewards.

Reaching a compromise is not the same as giving in. Compromise requires thought, patience and a pragmatic, philosophical approach – all the things you are best placed to contribute Taurus.

Working around the problem rather than clashing with it head-to-head will put you in a much better position to deepen your understanding. You may even gain a new vantage point, and from there you may be able to see new opportunities heading your way.

You are usually so measured
and calm Taurus, it can be a slightly
unpleasant surprise to those around
you when you find yourself a little,
shall we say, out of control. Be mindful
that, in venting your frustrations, you
don't negatively impact someone else.
You will likely feel better for getting it
off your chest, but there is a chance
they might feel a whole lot worse.

You are such a generous and giving person Taurus, that when the time comes to speak up for what you want for yourself, it can take others by surprise. Take this as a sign that you should do it more often, rather than feeling bad about it.

Following your feelings right
now will introduce a lot more focus
and direction into your life. You may
feel compelled to make changes.

With the gift of diplomacy (which you have by the bucketful Taurus) and not too much focus on the details, you will have this one solved to everyone's satisfaction in no time at all.

Acknowledge what you are feeling,
but at the same time understand that
it might not be all about the present.
Your subconscious has a way of
tapping you on the shoulder every
now and again to remind you of things
you have not yet dealt with.

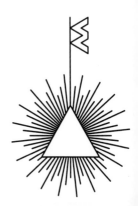

Stubborn or certain Taurus?
The interpretation depends on the
one making the judgement; do not
concern yourself with the opinions of
others when you know you are
doing the right thing.

Your dependability and dedication
can lead some more opportunistic
signs to consider you an easy source
of output and ideas... which they may
not then perhaps remember to credit
to you. Adopt a clean, straightforward
approach to nipping this in the bud.

If you are sensing negativity and bad energy, whatever form it takes, protect yourself with a little distance.

Taurus is a fixed modality sign, meaning that you are dependable, secure and will not be easily distracted from the task at hand. As an Earth sign, you also have your feet firmly planted. Rely on your pragmatic and stable nature now to come up with the easiest, least dramatic solution possible; it may not be the most exciting but will certainly be best for all concerned.

You value consistency and honesty high above most other character traits, and with good reason. If you suspect someone is not being straight with you or is adopting underhand techniques to sneak their way into first place, take a big step back. You don't want to be caught up in the inevitable fallout.

Taurean tenacity is a reliable feature
of your star-sign; when coupled with
your ambition and your love of reward,
it makes you an unstoppable force
once you have set your heart on your
goal. Draw on these gifts now
but use them wisely.

Resisting change comes naturally to you Taurus, and often activates a knee-jerk response rather than careful consideration. Has this happened again this time? Weigh up the options and likely outcomes here and apply some clean thinking to any resulting opportunities.

Just like your bullish constellation, you do have something of a reputation for being set in your ways. Open your eyes and your mind to the positives that revising your position might bring your way.

When emotions are flowing close to the skin's surface, the best approach is to maintain a happy, easy energy that helps to maintain movement and dissuade sinking or stagnation.
Keep it light.

Hard-working and pleasure-loving are two Taurean facets that complement each other particularly well. Putting in the time and effort will culminate in the kinds of rewards you adore.

Relaxing is important to you,
but you are never one to avoid the
work that must be done first – laziness
is definitely not a habit you are familiar
with. Right now, though, it is time to
assess whether the effort versus
reward equation is as balanced as
you would like it to be.

Positives and rewards are
winging their way towards you Taurus;
make sure you allow yourself the time
and headspace to really enjoy them.
You deserve it.

Dedicated and hard-working
as you are, it is essential that you find
balance with some excitement and
time for letting go Taurus. Burning out
right now would be a slippery slope.

Switching off to the world
outside for a little while is sometimes
an essential tactic for recharging
Taurus. Although you might worry
about letting someone down, in all
likelihood they will not feel that way.
And the big plus is that you will soon
be back up and running.

Honesty is one of your core values Taurus, and you are suspicious of secrecy. Allow others the benefit of the doubt here though; they may have very good reasons for keeping information close to their chests.

When those you love, or those close to you, see the benefits from their own hard work and ingenuity, you should feel pleased for them and proud of yourself as well Taurus. You have very likely been the role-model they needed.

Capable and respected as you are Taurus, you do not always have all the answers. In a time of uncertainty, or plain not-knowing, own up quickly to this gap in your knowledge.

You may not necessarily see yourself as creative Taurus, but creativity presents in many different forms. Right now, your ability to problem-solve and to craft a beautiful solution will definitely qualify you to join the creativity crowd.

Those you love will be with you every step of the way as you face this next set of challenges. You are not alone.

Allowing some space to breathe
in between your personal life and
your work focus is a crucial survival
technique Taurus, especially for
someone so dedicated. You will
not be the only one to benefit.

Emotional knots can take a long
while to untangle Taurus, and you
know you like to do things properly.
Take it slowly and ask for help
if you need it.

Intuition can be both a blessing and a curse. Luckily, you are not given to acting impulsively; be careful not to turn too quickly with this one.

Check in honestly with yourself
to be sure you are not sacrificing too
much. You will need to prioritize where
to best spend your efforts.

Others must manage their own
lives and that means making their
own mistakes and learning their own
lessons. There is only so much help
you can give before you are actually
doing them a disservice. Focus
on yourself Taurus.

Everything can be made to look good by positioning it alongside something worse. Judge this situation on its own merits rather than by comparing.

Correcting a misunderstanding
should be top of your list today Taurus
– once everything is straightened out,
then you will be able to see the way
ahead much more clearly.

Some may struggle to grasp the logic behind your decision. Be sure you are communicating your reasoning clearly.

Known for your intelligence
and wisdom, combined with an
analytical approach and a love of
fairness, you are often the first port of
call for a friend in need of advice. Be
sure you bring the same level of
concentration to finding solutions
to your own problems.

Indulging in self-celebration
can sometimes antagonise others...
even if that was the opposite of your
intention. Not everyone has the
generosity of spirit to enjoy the
successes of others. Perhaps it
might be best to downplay your
achievements for the time being.

Resist the urge to rush about Taurus; thundering bullishly into things right now might not be as important as you think. Relax, and take some time to be thankful and proud of what you are achieving.

Allow your thinking brain to pause today, always planning your next move will mean you miss the moments that make the now. Focus on feelings and the familiar; allow your deeper Taurean wisdom to guide your moves.

Play it cool and take it easy on output, whether that means holding back on sharing your opinions, deciding not to spend money or resisting the urge to send lots of energy out in various directions. Pull back in a bit, conserve your resources.

Space and time are the best
remedies for a disagreement,
misunderstanding or argument Taurus.
Give yourself a cooling-off period, then
return to seek further understanding
and/or make amends.

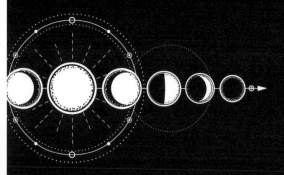

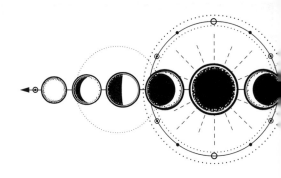

Your intuition is usually pitch
perfect Taurus – even if recently
you've been wondering whether it's
quite so finely tuned as it used to be.
Hold on to your confidence to lead
you through the next stage.

Keen as you are to get this one sorted out Taurus, you must resist the urge to move blindly forwards without preparation. Be sure you have checked your facts before you proceed.

Time to take a big swig of Taurus courage, there is some plain-speaking to be done now to clear up confusion arising from a few little white lies that have been creeping in recently.

Making the right choices is a
fine balance between heart and head
for you Taurus; go with what feels
right, even if your ultimate decision
takes you slightly by surprise.

You might find that plans and schedules you thought set in stone are suddenly all upside down. Everything is subject to change and revised arrangements are to be expected and embraced.

When your creative energy is jumping, allow it to run so you can see what happens next Taurus. Your dreams and imagination will expand your mind and give you access to new vistas you might never have known existed. Your problem-solving abilities will increase massively.

Maintain a straightforward and honest approach to the people around you, 'and also towards yourself. Your feelings may guide you to choose an easy way around, so be sure you balance this with some clear and logical reasoning.

Friendships and relationships should evolve naturally and slowly at the moment Taurus. Don't force intimacy (of any sort) too early, and don't allow yourself to be rushed by anyone else either.

Feeling angry as an escape from uncertainty or sadness is not a positive option Taurus. If you, or someone you are close to, seems to be struggling with anger you should call in some serious care and support.

Support others, particularly those
you care about, in following their
chosen direction without judgement.
If they request your opinion or advice,
offer it from a place of love and guide
them to make their own decisions.

Cancelling or rescheduling because something else comes up is not your style and something you avoid at all costs Taurus. But if you find now that there's nothing else for it, be upfront about presenting your dilemma and your decision. You may be surprised how well the other party takes it.

If you find yourself distracted right now, go with it. Perhaps your subconscious is drawing your attention to something you might otherwise not notice.

Resist the urge to hurry
headlong at things Taurus; if you
are in a constant rush you may miss
the most important details.

Let your super-busy brain take a break now and then Taurus, staying sharp and pinpoint-focused at all hours of the day and night is neither sustainable nor healthy. Embrace the drift and enjoy that sensation of relaxation as you go with the flow for a change.

Maintaining balance is essential Taurus; as a harmony-loving bull you know this perfectly well. While it might seem a difficult task, especially if there is conflict brewing, just keep your head down and do your bit.

Not every problem has a clean resolution Taurus; sometimes the fix can be just as messy to achieve as the issue was to create in the first place.

It is perfectly clear that the answer does not lie in the direction you thought. Stubbornness is to be avoided if possible Taurus, so resist following your ego's lead on this one.

Biding your time is the best option right now, and a sensible Taurus like you knows that. Turn your gaze inwards for a while or focus on something completely different.

Non-essential tasks can
wait for another day Taurus.

Allow your strong Taurean
intuition to take the lead on this and
read between the lines to understand
another's true intentions more clearly.
Build your response accordingly.

Slow down and step out of
the bustle today Taurus. With so
much going on and pressures seeming
to mount all the time, there is a danger
that you will miss out on what really
matters. Take some time to see things
differently, to breathe and to really
engage with the world around you.

Set aside the struggle for a
while Taurus; no point chasing
impossible dreams or trying to stitch
together irreparable rifts. Find
a task more worthy of your
not-inconsiderable talents.

Keep activity and movement at the forefront of everything you do right now Taurus. Maintaining the energy flow is definitely the way to go.

Determination and stoicism are
all very well Taurus, admirable traits
and all that, but they are not always
the best vehicles for delivering
happiness and light into your life. Keep
balance in mind at the moment
and seek out the beautiful, the
comfortable and the joyful.

If a particular challenge is cropping up at the moment, think carefully before accepting it (even though your bull-like instinct will be to challenge it straight back!). Will it really bring you the success you are looking for or is it another time-wasting distraction?

Strong-willed, enthusiastic and unwavering once you set on a course of action, you have everything you need already to hand Taurus. Step forwards to meet this one whole-heartedly and don't look back.

Have faith in yourself Taurus, your independent spirit, good judgement and clarity of approach mean that you are already well-equipped.

Speak your truth now Taurus;
there is no benefit to be gained
from biting your tongue any longer.
Keeping the peace is no reason to
increase your own inner turmoil.
Equilibrium will only be restored if you
are able to sort all this out, which
means you will need to talk about it.

Your gut instinct is strong and will help you find your way Taurus. Trust yourself.

Pare this one back to the essentials and don't draw any conclusions until the facts are all laid out. Sifting through, you may well find angles and options you hadn't previously considered.

Trying to force a solution that simply won't fit is a waste of your time and energy Taurus. You can see by now that this one probably won't budge, so stop pushing.

Set fear and uncertainty aside
Taurus, and find a way to push your
own limits out and away. You will
find that you are capable of much
more than you thought once you make
a conscious decision to challenge
the logic behind self-set constraints.

Information is everything Taurus, and without your ear to the ground you stand little chance of understanding what is really going on here. Don't be drawn in by idle gossip, but source some facts, do your groundwork and draw your own conclusions based on what you already know to be true.

Trying new things has got to be good for you Taurus, but be sure you are going in with the right attitude. Not all of it will work out, and you can't be an expert at everything you try. But you can learn plenty of useful things along the way and meet interesting new people, and you can have fun trying. Keep an open mind.

Being kind and accommodating
is one thing but being perceived as a
pushover is something completely
different. There is no need to stamp
and snort, but do respect the bull
within; don't bend further than you are
comfortable and hold your ground.

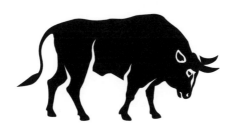

If somebody who is in, or who craves, a position of power is trying to work around you, it's essential you make it clear just how capable and determined you are. They will need to adapt to you Taurus. If you are forced into a defensive posture, be mindful it cannot be perceived as aggressive.

Use heightened energy to fuel greater productivity – getting more done now will be of tremendous benefit further down the road. Your enthusiasm and positivity may well have a major impact on others and this will bounce back to you in turn; spreading the love is all upside.

Options will spring up along
your path as you adopt a warm and
encouraging attitude to others around
you Taurus. If they are trying to turn
to you as a leader, allow it. You have all
the skills and traits necessary to
do the job extremely well.

Staying active is more important than ever Taurus – maintaining energy flow in the right direction will keep everything on track for a positive result.

Choosing a new direction for
your journey will lead you to a positive
place and bring new learning along
the way as well. Taking more risks
may mean you fail now and again,
but whether you are winning or not,
every experience will provide a
valuable lesson.

Tuning in to your emotions can be a lot trickier than it sounds, even for you Taurus. Sometimes, all runs smoothly; other times, not so much... If you are busy and distracted, you might not have had the chance to really examine the source of your unease. But it is important you get to grips with this one.

Impatience and increased anger could signal that you are feeling out of step with those around you Taurus. Excuse yourself from the crowd for a while, to take some much-needed rest and gain some perspective.

Resentment and indignation
are not familiar states to you Taurus;
you tend not to waste time on
emotions that are so obviously self-
destructive and limiting. If you feel this
kind of negativity creeping in, confront
it head on and deal with it early, to
prevent it growing to an
unhealthy size.

The more informed you are,
the better you will be able to handle
whatever this situation might throw at
you Taurus. Make use of the practical
determination your Earth sign has
gifted you with to work out everything
you need to know. Then get
on with finding out.

If a particular person has been a source of confrontation recently, be the bigger bull and suggest a frank and honest conversation about what has been going on. Whatever happens afterwards, you will have done the right thing by suggesting you talk.

We all change our minds sometimes Taurus, but you might have surprised even yourself with a recent abrupt about-turn. You're growing as a person, so it shouldn't be a shock that your ideas are changing too. If others are surprised or are asking you to justify yourself, you are more than ready.

Irritation or increased snappiness may be a sign of depression or exhaustion. If you are worried about such symptoms, in yourself or someone you are close to, make the time to look into coping strategies that might help and talk it through with others.

Giving others a hand up,
holding the door open, being
generous with your wisdom and your
expertise – these are all things you do
as naturally as breathing Taurus. Don't
consider changing; even if it feels like
maybe the rewards don't always flow
in the right direction, remind yourself
that this path is not chosen
for personal gain.

New beginnings are exciting,
but it's important that you hold onto
the value of old connections and
previous experience Taurus. Don't
wipe the slate clean, there is no need
for a one-in, one-out policy.

Your patience and calm stability mean you are most often accompanied by a strong, balanced energy; this both attracts like-minded people and ensures that you remain grounded. Use your influence wisely; a peaceful harmony is within your grasp.

Time for some adventure and exploration Taurus. There is a big wide world out there waiting to be discovered, and much energy waiting to connect with your own. Good things will happen.

Connections are strong for you Taurus, and the rhythm of your life is such that opportunities to discover new friends or renew old contacts come around often. Remember to conduct yourself in a way you can be proud of later; you are bound to meet again one way or another.

Don't take others too seriously at the moment, or yourself for that matter. There's plenty of bluster about and people blow hot and cold all the time. Without serious intention supporting it, none of this has any real meaning.

Take it slow getting to know new people at the moment Taurus – there is plenty of time and no need to reveal everything immediately, promising though your connection might seem.

When you find yourself confronted
with the strong opinions of others ,
resist the urge to charge back with
bullish determination. Instead, look for
a route around the problem; it will be
much more efficient and expend far
less energy. Win win.

You mustn't allow yourself to
be rushed into something if your
intuition is telling you to take
your time. Other people's hurry is
their own problem; your commitment
is to doing things well and the right
way. Stick to your plans.

Focus can sometimes seem frustratingly elusive to you Taurus; for all that you are a practical, grounded type, there is a dreaminess that floats across from time to time – and it can be hard to shake. Rather than fighting it, go along with it. This softened view will bring fresh perspective.

Give your brain power the credit,
and the rejuvenation time, it deserves.
You will be depending on it almost
exclusively in the upcoming period –
do yourself a favour and take some
rest while you can.

The path of your life runs backwards and forwards, and through the present. Acknowledge how valuable your past has been in bringing you to where you are now and in shaping the way you will move forwards from here.

Staying head-down and task-oriented may seem more difficult than usual Taurus. Perhaps there is a reason for this, something your memory is trying to bring up to the top of your consciousness? Either way, you will need to work with your energy the way it is. Try parcelling everything into smaller, more manageable chunks and building in plenty of breaks.

If you are finding your
energy low and motivation
at a minimum, it is a sign that you
need some nourishment, some rest,
some downtime. Turning inwards
when you can is a great solution,
whether for just a few minutes with
some music or by switching off your
phone and spending an afternoon
in bed. You will be back to
yourself in no time.

Don't be tempted to engage
with others on an important issue
until you have your facts straight. Most
likely, some of them will genuinely
know something and others are simply
enjoying the sound of their own
voices. Either way, hold your integrity
and bypass the bluster.

It may feel that someone or
something is circling at the moment,
not in a predatory way, but more
taking stock, weighing you up, working
you out. You should be taking the
opportunity to evaluate them
(or it) as well.

Watch the way you are communicating Taurus – could your tone be misinterpreted or your questioning misunderstood? Be mindful of how others you are engaging with might be hearing you.

With your bullish mindset, it can sometimes prove tricky to ascertain whether you are facing a real difficulty or simply absorbing a troublesome energy from somewhere else. Stick to the facts right now Taurus, and be prepared to change your mind if anything new comes to light.

Communication is a strong channel
with you bulls, but sometimes the line
between truth and tact can be rubbed
up against so often it becomes a little
blurry. Be as diplomatic as possible
without muddying your message.

While you might find it difficult to retain your patience with complainers at the moment Taurus, take the time to consider whether there might be a productive way to think around the issues that are being flagged. Others could also benefit.

You are something of a magnet for interesting contacts Taurus, and deservedly so. Take your time really getting to know some of the new people who have been showing up in your space recently.

Sorting out any niggles or glitches
in relationships should take priority for
you now Taurus – the repercussions
of issues left unaddressed may
be far-reaching.

If someone close to you (either emotionally or proximally) seems to be carrying a heavier-than-usual load, reach out and see what help you might be able to offer.

When emotions overload
your headspace, you may find your
own behaviour surprising. Other
people might be finding you
unpredictable, too. Spend a while
looking at what's going on within
and offering your true self
some support.

Take courage Taurus; if a conversation requires starting it might be that you have to be the one to speak the first words.

You have the opportunity to make some real progress now Taurus. Don't shy away from the potentially weighty issues that require your attention.

Let the emotions rise up rather than suppressing them Taurus; while they might feel uncomfortable in the moment, allowing them within the process is all part of the important work you are doing right now.

Miscommunication doesn't
always need to be straightened out
immediately Taurus. Take a pragmatic
approach to this one and remember
that responding graciously will
take you a long way.

Load management is crucial
at the moment Taurus; identify the
secondary tasks that can wait while
you attend to more urgent issues.

If you are feeling bold and ready
to make a change, now is the time to
take a risk Taurus. Pass this one over
to chance and see what happens.

Don't allow the strong personalities and opinions of others to pin you in place Taurus; everyone is entitled to their own ways of thinking and being, and that includes you. Allow, acknowledge and keep moving.

Connecting to your own truth is
essential to maintain your own
grounded sense of strength.

If developments or conversations create an uncomfortable atmosphere Taurus, you are under no obligation to stay. Make your excuses and slip smoothly away.

Fall back on your instincts
and intuition as you communicate
with others Taurus. Listen carefully for
the pauses and watch the way things
are said. Is something important
remaining unspoken? Are there
avoidance techniques at play? Trust
your eyes and your gut as much as
your ears right now.

Commit to your own health and
wellbeing Taurus – there is plenty
more you can do to enhance
your own self-care regime.

If conversations seem to be taking on an unwelcome air of intensity Taurus, take a pause and try a different approach. Remember, communication is not just about what people say; pay close attention.

Don't wait for others to ask you
for help if you can see that
your assistance is required Taurus;
be proactive.

When tensions arise, try to keep a close check on your own emotions and resist too volatile a reaction. No matter how much relief a little irritation-release might give you in the short term, it's unlikely to pay off in the long run.

First published in Great Britain in 2021 by
Greenfinch
An imprint of Quercus Editions Ltd
Carmelite House
50 Victoria Embankment
London EC4Y 0DZ

An Hachette UK company

A CIP catalogue record for this book is available
from the British Library.

HB ISBN 978-1-52941-230-7

10 9 8 7 6 5 4 3

Designed by Ginny Zeal
Cover design by Andrew Smith
Text by Susan Kelly
All images from Shutterstock.com

Printed and bound in China.

Papers used by Greenfinch are from well-managed forests
and other responsible sources.